50 Recipes of Butters and Vegan Mayonnaise

Delicious and healthy alternatives to traditional recipes

NELY HELENA ACOSTA CARRILLO

50 Recipes of Butters and Vegan Mayonnaise

Delicious and healthy alternatives to traditional recipes

Nely Helena Acosta Carrillo

All the biblical verses used in this book have been extracted from the Bible in its King James Version.
All the quotes of the North American writer Elena G. White (EGW) have been extracted from the books published by the different Publishing Houses owned by the Seventh-day Adventist Church: PACIFIC PRESS, APIA, ACES, GEMA EDITORES, SAFELIZ.

Title of the book in Spanish: 50 Recetas de Mantequillas y Mayonesas veganas

English translation: Jared Acosta Carrillo and Nely Helena Acosta Carrillo
Cover design: Jared Acosta Carrillo
Photography, photo editing, design and layout: Jared Acosta Carrillo

To contact the author:
E-mail: nelyacosta05@hotmail.com
YouTube Channel: SALUD A LA CARTA (Spanish channel)
Facebook: nelyhelena.acostacarrillo
Instagram: nelyacosta_saludalacarta
Twitter: SALUD A LA CARTA @CartaSalud

50 Recipes of Butters and Vegan Mayonnaise
© Nely Helena Acosta Carrillo
Year: 2019

E-book ISBN: 978-1-7923-1811-5

Published by NELY ACOSTA & QUINONES PUBLICATIONS, LLC.

TABLE OF CONTENTS

Words of gratitude — 11
Dedicated to — 13
Biblical verse — 15
Changing eating habits: an urgent need — 17
Traditional mayonnaise: a terrible combination of "foods" — 19
Traditional butter: a very toxic fat — 23
Margarine: almost plastic — 27
Things to consider — 33
Recipes — 41

Vegan Butters — 43

Coconut oil and olive oil butter — 45
Cashew and spinach butter — 46
Sunflower seed butter — 47
Pumpkin seed butter — 48
Pistachio butter — 49
Chickpea butter — 50
Tofu and tempeh butter — 51
Dried tomato butter — 52
Eggplant butter — 53
Zucchini and onions butter — 54
Green olives butter — 55
Avocado and dried tomato butter — 56
Brazil nut and apricots butter — 57
Almond and prunes butter — 58

Peanut and honey butter 59
Peanut and raisins butter 60
Peanut and dates butter 61
Fig and nut butter 62
Hazelnut and pineapple butter 63
Berries and cashews butter 64
Macadamia nut and dates butter 65
Chia seed, berries and prunes butter 66
Dry coconut and sesame butter 67
Tender coconut meat and carob flour butter 68
Pumpkin and carob flour butter 69

Vegan Mayonnaise — 71

Tofu mayonnaise 73
Tofu and coriander mayonnaise 74
Asparagus mayonnaise 75
Black olives mayonnaise 76
Fine herbs mayonnaise 77
Lentil mayonnaise 78
Basil mayonnaise 79
Avocado and peppermint mayonnaise 80
Avocado and mint mayonnaise 81
Avocado and coriander mayonnaise 82
Almond mayonnaise 83
Cashew mayonnaise 84
Cashew and spirulina mayonnaise 85
Spinach and Brazil nut mayonnaise 86
Red peppers and almonds mayonnaise 87

Zucchini and pumpkin seeds mayonnaise — 88
Zucchini and oregano mayonnaise — 89
Soft yogurt mayonnaise — 90
Garlic mayonnaise — 91
Beet mayonnaise — 92
Tomato mayonnaise — 93
Carrot mayonnaise — 94
Potato and radish mayonnaise — 95
Celery and walnut mayonnaise — 96
Cauliflower mayonnaise — 97

My wish for you — 99

Words of gratitude

To God,
who has taught me things
that I didn't know before and that
have allowed to improve in
superlative grade the quality of
life of my loved ones, and also mine.

Dedicated to

To all who wish to be able
to live a better life.

"Whether therefore ye eat, or drink, or whatsoever ye do, do all to the glory of God."

1 Corinthians 10:31

Changing eating habits: an urgent need

The people are sick. It is estimated that approximately 90% of the prayers raised each week in the churches are in favor of the sick people inside and outside the church. That speaks of a terrible health situation worldwide. The church is sick, and the community is too. On the other hand, medical statistics ensure that between 70-80% of patients worldwide are suffering from the so-called acute, chronic and degenerative diseases. These diseases are directly related to the lifestyle, or, rather, to the bad lifestyle. The lifestyle encompasses all our physical habits, and they all have a brutal impact on people's health.

Habits or lifestyle range from trust in divine power, which avoids stress, a silent enemy of modern man, to breathe fresh air, eat healthy, drink water, sunbathe, exercise, rest, dress properly, be in a friendly environment and be temperate in all areas of life. All of that are part of the lifestyle. However, today it is known that eating habits are within the lifestyle factors that most determine the health of people. In fact, as Dr. Paul White rightly states: "Most health problems begin in the kitchen." Not for pleasure in the Bible, the instruction manual for all human beings, God, who is our creator, our redeemer, who sustains us, and who heals us, gives us a touch of attention when he says: "Wherefore I pray you to take some meat: for this is for your health."[1] That means that there is a way of eating that gives

---
[1] Acts 27:34

health, but that there is another that doesn't just give it to us, but he also steals the one we have.

Poor quality fats, such as those used to make mayonnaises, butters and margarines, are part of that bad eating that is taking away people's health. The cardio and cerebrovascular problems that result from the intake of these anti-physiological, dirty and acidifying "foods", in addition to diabetes, obesity, metabolic syndrome or cancer, just to name a few of the hundreds of diseases that prevail in our day by day, are taking a toll without mercy. Every day, more and more people, big and small, are sick. With great foundation the statistics affirm that more than 95% of the world population has health problems, and that more than a third have more than five illness. People's health is in crisis. Physical and mental exhaustion is a reality in more and more lives. And bad food is at the base of all that. It is hard to understand that in order to enjoy health "those foods should be chosen that best supply the elements needed for building up the body. In this choice, appetite is not a safe guide. Through wrong habits of eating, the appetite has become perverted. Often it demands food that impairs health and causes weakness instead of strength. We cannot safely be guided by the customs of society. The disease and suffering that everywhere prevail are largely due to popular errors in regard to diet."[2] And in the universe, there is the law of cause and effect, and decisions count, so, "the food you eat can be the most powerful form of medicine or the slowest form of poison."[3]

Well, having seen it, I invite you to take a closer look at what traditional mayonnaise, butter and margarita recipes offer. Informing yourself is very important in order to become aware of the imperative need for a change in eating habits in an irrevocable, permanent and urgent way. However, having knowledge is not enough. Each person must make use of their free will and their ability to choose and decide whether or not they want to learn to eat in a better way in order to avoid so many ailments that swarm in the world today. But, without a doubt, it is our privilege to use the wise biblical advice that states: "Seek good, not evil, so that you may live; because thus the Lord of hosts will be with you."[4]

---

[2] EGW. The Ministry of Healing. 295
[3] Ann Wigmore (March 4, 1909 – February 16, 1994) was a lithuanian-american holistic health practitioner and raw food advocate.
[4] Amos 5:14

Traditional mayonnaise: a terrible combination of "foods"

Mayonnaise, a preparation of Spanish origin (from Menorca island, Spain), is a cold emulsified sauce made mainly from egg yolk and refined vegetable oils, both shakes. Traditionally, it has been seasoned with salt and vinegar, and made by hand. Nowadays things have changed significantly, and that sauce is made at an industrial level, not homemade, and its consumption is mainly associated with junk food or fast food, although, it is also used in many international dishes as an accompaniment, including vegetables, rice, pasta and fish.

There are curiosities surrounding this recurring creamy dressing. Have you ever wondered how much mayonnaise you could get with just one egg yolk? Well, in his book The Curious Cook, its author, Harold McGee, writer specializing in culinary issues, responds to that dilemma. He discovered that more than 22 liters. But, in addition, there is another question: Did you know which is the molecule that allows the egg and the oil to emulsify to form the mayonnaise? Because we all know that water and oil are immiscible, said in other words, no matter how much we shake them: they don't mix. Well, the only way to get both to become friends is through the work of mediators. And these mediators are surfactant molecules that fulfill a double function: on the one hand, they are attracted to water, and, on the other, to oil. It is thanks to them that you can make mayonnaise, which is nothing more than an emulsion. In chemistry, one speaks of an emulsion when one liquid disperses in another in the form of small droplets. Who provides that glue is the egg yolk, a basic ingredient of traditional mayonnaise, which contains substances such as lecithin, which are phospholipids that are responsible for coating the oil drops. At the same time, these coated droplets do not bond with each other because the surfactants are electrically charged and repel. That explains why vinegar is used in the preparation. What happens is that in an acidic medium the surfactant molecules have a greater load and repel with greater intensity. Only then can a sauce like mayonnaise be achieved.

But there is a third curiosity regarding traditional mayonnaise, and it also comes in the form of a question: why is mayonnaise broken? The answer is simple. The mechanical effect of beating mayonnaise has a very clear objective: to break the oil into smaller and smaller droplets and distribute them through the water. It is the reason that explains why the oil is added slowly, little by little, and not at once. When the mayonnaise is broken it is because the procedure used has not been able to achieve the proper dispersion of the oil. In technical terms, when that happens, it is claimed that the mixture has flocculated, that is, the drops of oil come together and separate from the water. And that happens when the ingredients are too cold or when the egg yolk has not provided enough water for the amount of oil used in the recipe. To fix the problem it is usually recommended to add another egg yolk to the mixture, 50% of an egg yolk is water, or add a little water and beat again vigorously.

The technical-sanitary regulation establishes that for a product to be classified as mayonnaise it must contain a minimum of 65% of vegetable oil and 5% of egg yolk, so we are talking about an extremely fatty sauce, and, therefore, harmful to body health.

In conclusion, traditional mayonnaise - whether industrial or homemade - is one of the worst "foods" that exist. Its combination of ingredients is absolutely insane. The level of overfermentation and acidity caused by the consumption of this badly called food in the body, over the years, even at the most resistant bodies, sooner or later, ends up taking them to the hospital. How is mayonnaise made? With egg yolk (a product loaded with hormones, antibiotics and cholesterol), refined sunflower oil (saturated with carcinogens due to the manufacturing process to which it is subjected), refined salt (loaded with chloride and sodium, two minerals that used in this way can trigger blood pressure), and vinegar (water miscible liquid, with a sour taste, which comes from the acetic fermentation of alcohol and is highly acidifying). Traditional mayonnaise is one of the worst combinations that exist under the sun. It is almost impossible to imagine something that could be worse for the cardiovascular system. With such ingredients you can perfectly prepare a good nuclear bomb. The formula of traditional mayonnaise is like the formula of death:

Egg + Refined oil + Refined Salt + Vinegar

In order to be healthy, you must be safe from formulas like this.

However, it is incredible to see that despite the harmful effects on health on the consumption of traditional mayonnaise, whether industrial or homemade, in this world there are true lovers of mayonnaise. Even in 2010, the Ukrainian Oleg Zhornitskiy won the Guinness Prize for eating 4 pots of mayonnaise of one liter each in just 8 minutes. There is no doubt that we live in a world where good is called bad, and bad is called good.

Now, do you have to deprive yourself of eating mayonnaise? No, you don't have to give it up. But it is not necessary to consume this harmful combination having healthy ways to enjoy a homemade mayonnaise, free of chemicals and full of nutrition that can delights your palate. The wisest and recommended decision is to move towards mayonnaise options that break with the traditional recipe, and that have among their ingredients true foods that not only satisfy the most demanding palates, but also can be convenient for general health.

TRADITIONAL MAYONNAISE

 Delicious

but

 Deadly

Traditional mayonnaise

= **Refined oil** (Full of petroleum-derived carcinogens)

\+ **Egg** (With abundant cholesterol, hormones, antibiotics and other toxins)

\+ **Refined salt** (Loaded with sodium, one of the worst enemies of cardiovascular health)

\+ **Vinegar** (It comes from the acetic fermentation of alcohol and is highly acidifying, even if it is apple vinegar)

Traditional mayonnaise, whether industrial or homemade, is ideal for acidifying the body. Acidification creates inflammation, and both are the basis of all acute, chronic and degenerative diseases that plague us today, among which 70-80% of patients worldwide are grouped. Traditional mayonnaise is not food. It is poison. It does not provide health, but weakens, sickens and even kills your body.

Traditional butter: a very toxic fat

Butter, also known as fat, according to the experts opinions, is the emulsion of fat, water and milk solids obtained as a result of beating, kneading and washing the conglomerates of fatty globules that are formed by whipping the cream of milk, with or without the biological maturation produced by specific lactic bacteria, and considered suitable for human consumption.

According to history, one of the first people that made butter were the Mongols, the Celts and the Vikings. They obtained this as a result of the kneading of the cream of the milk of different mammals, especially cows, sheep and goats. Initially, the Greeks and Romans cataloged butter as, and I literally quote, "food for barbarians," and it made its consumption not spread throughout Europe until the fourteenth century. From then on, butter became part of the usual foods of the population in America, Oceania and Asia. The invention of the centrifuge[5] at the end of the 19th century, of pasteurization[6], and the increase of knowledge

---

[5] Centrifuge: Machine that allows to separate the cream from the milk more quickly.
[6] Pasteurization: A procedure that involves subjecting a food, usually liquid, to an approximate temperature of 80°C (176°F), for a short period of time, and then cooling it quickly, in order to destroy the microorganisms without altering the composition and qualities of the liquid.

regarding the use of certain bacteria in food, allowed the butter to begin to be produced at an industrial level.

To elaborate the butter industrially the following process is followed. First, the milk is pasteurized, which consists of heating it at a temperature between 92 and 95°C (197.6 and 203°F), for half of a minute. In this way - at least in theory - the bacteria considered as possible disease-generating pathogens are destroyed and the lipases are inactivated. The lipases are enzymes that are present in the milk. They are directly responsible for certain serious alterations in the butter detected during the storage process. In order to favor the crystallization of fat and improve its extensibility, pasteurized milk is left at rest at low temperatures. Subsequently, lactic ferments are added for a period of fifteen hours, maintaining a temperature between 14 and 16°C (57.2 and 60.8°F) with the purpose of promoting the production of lactic acid, responsible for providing the characteristic aroma and acidity of the butter. To finish the process, the cream fat is beaten hard, which turns it into butter. Then, you may or may not add salt. It is cleaned with sterile pure water and kneaded to achieve a uniform distribution.

For the butter to be considered top quality the dough must be compact, not very hard, and must have a yellow color. It is known that its contact with the air makes it easily rancid, and that affects its quality standards. In order that it does not lose its properties, it must be preserved from heat, light and air.

On the other hand, it is worth mentioning that there are several types of butter, but they are mainly grouped into two categories:

- Acid butter: after the acidification of the cream. This is the traditional one.
- Sweet butter: before the acidification of the cream.

In addition, as already mentioned, you can add salt or not, obtaining salted or normal butter, depending on the case. And, of course, it can be made from the milk of many animals. The most common in the West are sheep, cow or goat butter. As a curiosity I mention that it is not possible to obtain butter from camel milk.

Traditional butter, from the nutritional point of view, is a product with a high fat content, and fats of the worst quality. One hundred grams of butter contain between eighty and eighty-five grams of fat, of which, approximately, sixty grams are saturated fatty acids, twenty-five grams are monounsaturated fatty acids, and only two grams are polyunsaturated fatty acids. On the other hand, one hundred grams of butter contain two hundred and thirty milligrams of cholesterol. The amounts of vitamin A and D, calcium, phosphorus, sodium, potassium and magnesium present in that popular dairy derivative are minimal.

Like mayonnaise, despite how harmful it can be, traditional butter, whether homemade or industrial, is widely consumed by most people. But, this type of mistakenly called "food" has never been part of God's dietary plan for humanity. He knew that the consumption of that type of fat conflicts with people's health. In fact, although there is not a single biblical verse that explicitly prohibits eating butter, the English Dictionary defines butter as the fatty portion of milk, separating as a soft whitish or yellowish solid when milk or cream is agitated or churned. The question is: what command Jehovah of Armies to his people when with great power He freed them from the slave yoke of ancient Egypt, and gave him the dietary rules they should follow? The answer comes to us through a biblical verse, and, although that biblical verse was written thousands of years ago, the contents of his letters speak loud and clear today: "Speak unto the children of Israel, saying, Ye shall eat no manner of fat, of ox, or of sheep, or of goat."[7] Well, it turns out that butter is one of the most toxic fats we can consume. It is the beaten fat of cow's milk. And while it is true that the use of butter by the people of God was an habitual practice at that time, as is confirmed by some biblical passages,[8] that does not mean that it was something that would cheer the heart of the Creator, because its consumption is openly against the food standards that God himself stipulated.

Butter intake is not good for anyone, but, like is logic, due to its high percentage of saturated fat and cholesterol, its consumption is contraindicated especially for people who are overweight, obese, hypercholesterolemia, hypertriglyceridemia, diabetes, and cardiovascular and sight disorders.[9]

Finally, "we know that cheap fats such as soybean oil, canola oil or corn oil (refined), are not healthy to consume in large quantities, in the long term. The worst type of fats are the partially hydrogenated. They are the hydrogenated oils used in baked foods such as cookies, butters, margarines, whipped butters, etc. Those are the worst products you can eat. If you want healthy fats you need to eat natural fats that you find in avocados, chia seeds, flaxseed. Those are healthy fats."[10] Butter is the pure and concentrated fat of the

---

[7] Leviticus 7:23

[8] "Brought beds, and basons, and earthen vessels, and wheat, and barley, and flour, and parched corn, and beans, and lentiles, and parched pulse, and honey, and butter, and sheep, and cheese of kine, for David, and for the people that were with him, to eat: for they said, The people is hungry, and weary, and thirsty, in the wilderness." 2 Samuel 17:28-29

[9] "Cataracts are also linked to dairy products. Galactose also damages the eye's lenses, causing cataracts." Digestive Disease and Sciences. 1982; 27: 257-64.

"According to one study, butter is the food that most increases the risk of cataracts, when consumed regularly." Roger. D. Pamplona MD. Health for food, 31. Editorial Safeliz. Madrid. Spain.

[10] Mike Adams. Nutrition Master. Health journalist and writer. Hungry for change (a North American documentary about nutrition and weight loss made in 2012).

cow's milk. It is one of the most toxic fats we can eat. That is not convenient for anyone. And much less for you.

Margarine: almost plastic

The English Dictionary defines margarine as a butterlike product made of refined vegetable oils, sometimes blended with animal fats, and emulsified, usually with water or milk. Margarine is a trans-fat, that means, transformed. Trans-fats are a type of food fat. This fat are formed when food manufacturers convert liquid oils into solid fats, such as margarine, using the hydrogenation or hydrogen injection process to solidify them. Trans-fats are found in many fried foods, in fast food and in packaged or processed foods, such as breaded and fried foods, margarine, cakes, cake mix, pie, pie dough, etc. Animal foods, such as red meat and dairy, have small amounts of trans-fats, but most trans-fats come from processed foods.

Of all fats, trans-fats are one of the worst for your health. According to the archives of the National Library of Medicine of the United States, consuming too much trans-fat in the diet increases your risk of heart disease and other health conditions. Trans-fats increase your LDL (bad) cholesterol and lower your HDL (good) cholesterol and having high LDL levels and low HDL levels can cause cholesterol to build up in the blood vessels, especially in the arteries. This increases the chances of having heart diseases or even strokes. In addition, trans-fats promote weight gain and diabetes risk, and, unfortunately, many high-fat foods, such as baked goods and fried foods, have many trans-fats. Eating too much trans-fat can cause weight gain and may also increase your risk of developing type 2 diabetes. Maintaining a healthy weight can reduce your risk of diabetes, heart disease and other health problems.

When fat oxidizes, it creates free radicals. Trans-fats, such as margarine, are rancid and oxidized fats and create the proper ground for free radicals, which are the number one enemy of cells, to flood the system. These free radicals, of which cholesterol is a part, adhere to the walls of the arteries and capillaries and are very difficult to detach, and with an overwhelming ease they form the dreaded atheromatous plaques responsible of cardio and cerebral vascular problems, between many other health problems. And, to make matters worse, when that fat is combined with animal fats and proteins, they become a time bomb inside the body. Besides, oxidative stress is the process of cellular deterioration and it dependent of the production of free radicals. The excess of free radicals damage our body causing, at best, early aging, and at worst, serious diseases. People have the right to know that "everything that causes oxidative stress creates a free radical reaction, and free radicals will create damage to the individual's body tissue, and the body will try to defend you by trying to patch, and the patch is cholesterol. What causes oxidative stress? Refined vegetable oils and vegetable margarines, among other things. By the way, between the margarine and the butter – none one is recommended - the butter made of the milk of a healthy cow that feeds on grass is better, or, at least, if you don't give me the butter, don't give me the margarine either."[11] The margarine only serves to clean shoes. Margarine is so harmful that you would win if you used to eat or cook Vaseline instead of that almost piece of plastic. Margarine is very high in trans fatty acids, causes a triple risk of coronary heart disease, increases total cholesterol and LDL (bad cholesterol) and lowers HDL (good cholesterol), increases the risk of cancer by five times, it decreases the quality of breast milk, decreases the body's immune reaction and the reaction to insulin, just to name a few of the effects of its intake on the body. And watch out for deceptive advertising. "Margarine with 0% cholesterol will raise my cholesterol because it will cause oxidative damage, which in turn will cause me free radical damage, which in turn will force my liver to release and secrete more and more cholesterol."[12]

    Dr. Walter Julius Veith explains that "the American Society of Heart Diseases began warning against saturated fats and said they are the ones that cause heart disease. By 1970 the warning began to take effect and the average American began to change his diet and take more polyunsaturated fats and less saturated fats. They also said that it was better to switch from butter to margarine. From that moment, between 1970 to 1993, the number of heart attacks among the population was drastically reduced. It corresponds with the period in which the strong advertising campaign caused people to become aware and change their diet. Similar campaigns were raised around the world urging people to change from saturated to polyunsaturated fats to prevent heart disease. That was great. But what about fats and cancer? In that same period, while heart attacks went down, cancer grew. The number of people with breast and prostate cancer soared. What was the problem?

---

[11] Oscar Sande. Nutritionist. Nutrition and Vegetarianism Series: Principle and Application. Conference Number II. Published by ALFA TV. ALFA Total Health Association / 2013.
[12] Identical.

All nations that were high fat consumers were the ones with the highest cancer rates. So, in the 80s they began to do experiments and found that the diet is affected by what people eat, and especially, by the consumption of fats. So, the more fat a nation consumes, the higher the risk of cancer, especially of breasts, colon cancer, rectal cancer, prostate and pancreas cancer. Those are the types of cancer that are induced by fatty products."[13]

Margarines and hydrogenated oils have become one of the major health problems that we face today. What are the ingredients of margarine? Soybean, corn, sunflower, olive, coconut and palm oil, emulsifiers, colorants, preservatives and flavorings. That mixture of things goes through a process to eliminate insoluble gums and other elements, and by another procedure called neutralization for which caustic soda is used. From there it follows processes of bleaching, filtration, deodorization, hydrogenation -with a lot of heat and a hydrogen catalyst- and margarine is made. Vegetable oil is a liquid and is the main ingredient of margarine. The question is: So, how is margarine solid and not liquid if it comes from vegetable oil? Because a lot of hydrogen which has been added to achieve that solidification. "Vegetable oil has been transformed from liquid to solid because the industry knows that since margarine is a substitute for butter, the consumer does not want to be spilled on bread, what he wants is to spread it on bread. When the oil is transformed in this way by having gone through so many procedures, the bacteria do not have the enzymes that recognize the fat, which is good for the industry because it means that it is not going to get rancid. You know what? The new generations do not know what a stale food is. They do not know. When was the last time you heard that a food has gone rancid? That doesn't happen anymore. And why don't they get rancid? Because bacteria don't want it anymore. Why don't they want them anymore? Because they can't digest them anymore. The bad news is that these bacteria have the same enzymes as humans to digest those foods, which means we can't digest them well either. So, what is margarine really? It is a trans-fat, that is, transformed. It is a foreign substance. I call it shoe cream. It is good for cleaning shoes, but not for human consumption. The problem is that when people ingested them the body find a type of fat that is not able to digest. What can do with it? Store it where it does not bother, in the same way in which the junk of a home is stored in the attic of the house. So, the body stores it under the skin, and it begins to enter in the connective tissues making the typical lumps that identify cellulite. In that condition you begin to exercise strongly, but that cellulite will not disappear. The only way to get rid of it is to stop eating that almost plastic that is a trans-fat, and at the same time exercise. Over time it will go through the skin because the skin is oily, the cells will break, and the fat will be released that way and the problem will be solved."[14]

---

[13] Walter Julius Veith MD. Conference Your health, your choice.
[14] Identical.

Margarine, that trans-fat, has caused an epidemic of diseases in this society, including obesity. Please, understand it well: much of the industrial food contain margarine. Each time, more and more countries prohibit their consumption by imposing restrictions on their use by the food industry. The hydrogenation of vegetable oils that is applied to give them consistency and so that at room temperature these fats harden is a procedure that alters the natural molecules of vegetable oil, its main ingredient, and creates a highly carcinogenic substance. Currently, the egg has 15 times more Omega 6 than 3, but margarine has much more: 70 times more Omega 6 than 3. Omega 3 is anti-inflammatory, but Omega 6 is inflammatory. That is why its intake produces chronic inflammatory disorders, chronic pain, joint discomfort, fatigue, exhaustion and an absolute dislocation in the body. The consumption of margarine also weakens the immune system because the immune system does not identify it as food, but as foreign molecules. In fact, it is claimed that margarine only lacks one molecule to be a plastic. And, although in reality margarine is not plastic, since it is made from hydrogenated vegetable oils, the truth is that it has been discovered that it only lacks a chemical compound to become plastic, so we can say that eating margarine is almost the same as eating a piece of plastic. It is logical that before its presence in the body the immune system detects it as something rare and attacks it. But, once again, despite how dangerous it is, many people consume it. Margarine consumption has triggered the rates of obesity and inflammatory syndrome. Inflammation at low levels, but permanently, is the basis of all the acute, chronic and degenerative diseases that humanity suffers today, and among which most of the patients are grouped.

When the blanket is pulled to understand how margarine is made, what is found is creepy. As it turns out, "to the refined oil, already unusable, we add hydrogen and it becomes butter. Then, we paint it yellow, we salt it and it is called margarine. By eating margarine, we are eating hydrocarbons. An arepa made with Vaseline would possibly be less harmful than with margarine. (...) Almost all diseases are associated with the consumption of refined oils and margarines."[15]

If you want to lower cholesterol you should not eat margarine as a substitute for butter because margarine is a hydrogenated fat, that is, a trans-fat, and it has been proven that rises cholesterol even more than butter. In addition, hydrogenated fats, as is the case with margarines, have a lot of nickel, which, according to Dr. Hulda Clark's statements, is a potent carcinogen. Your body does not obtain any benefit from trans-fats. Eat those fats increases your risk of having health problems of all kinds.

Trans-fats, such as margarine, are not food, they are not suitable for human consumption. They never have been and never will be. They are not a nutriment. They are good for the industry, and the years have shown that what is good for the industry is bad

---

[15] Germán Alberti. Naturópata MD. Conference The laws of health.

for you. Even because it is known that margarine only lacks a chemical to be plastic, this fact should be enough to avoid its use or the use of any other "food" that contains hydrogenated oils, either totally or partially hydrogenated. Adding hydrogen artificially to these fats they changes their molecular structure, and that change does not benefit at all. Eating margarine is like eating Vaseline. They are bad fats painted yellow. The coveted margarine is unnatural and harmful to your body. And there is a way to see how harmful margarine is by oneself. How? Through a simple experiment. Buy some margarine and leave it uncovered in a shady place. Wait patiently and within a few days you will notice two things:

1- There will be no flies or any other living being perching on it. Not even those annoying bugs will approach it.
2- It does not rot or smell bad or different because it has no nutritional value. Nothing grows in it. Not even the tiny microorganisms can grow there. Not even bacteria want it.

Why does that happen? Because margarine is almost plastic, and neither animals nor microorganisms perceive it as food.

Conclusion? As human beings the intake of margarine does not suit us.

One is poison. The other too.

Butter

Margarine

VS

When asked what is healthier, if butter or margarine, the answer is as follows: If we keep in mind that the first one is full of saturated fats and cholesterol, and that the second one is abundant in hydrogenated fats and trans fatty acids, the answer is obvious:

NONE.

It's a question if you wanna be shot or hanged.
If one is harmful, the other is worse.

Things to consider

All the recipes shared in this book, both, butter and vegan mayonnaise, have been designed to be able to substitute in the best possible way the traditional recipes that, in terms of health, do not bring any benefit. All of them are free of animal products, fats and toxic proteins, refined products and chemical additives. All preparations can not only be considered true foods, but also authentic medicines, because they are full of products of the earth in their most virgin state and loaded with vitamins, minerals, fats and proteins of the highest quality and biologically convenient, complete carbohydrates, phytochemicals, enzymes and fiber, and those are precisely the best foods. And, when we talk about replacing mayonnaises, butters and margarines with better options, we are talking mainly from the nutritional point of view. As for taste, smell and texture there is nothing in this world that can imitate the detail of mayonnaise, butter or traditional margarine. We are talking about a different concept of food, of a superior form of food, and considering that, "when properly prepared, olives, like nuts, supply the place of butter and flesh meats,"[16] various recipes of this volume have as the main ingredients precisely these foods. In fact, for example, "olives may be so prepared as to be eaten with good results at every meal. The advantages sought by the use of butter may be obtained by the eating of properly prepared olives. The oil in the olives relieves constipation, and for consumptives, and for those who have inflamed, irritated stomachs, it is better than any drug. As a food it is better than any oil coming secondhand from animals."[17] Mayonnaises and butters made with nuts, dried fruits, seeds, legumes and other products of the earth, are a true feast of nutrients, have an exquisite flavor and they are an immense source of energy for the body.

Note that some of the recipes shared in this edition contain ingredients that maybe are not familiar to some people, so they are detailed below in order the reader can familiarize with them:

- **The Herbes de Provence (in French):** It is a natural seasoning. It is made up of a mixture of dry and native culinary plants from the Mediterranean areas, and especially from Provence, a region located in the south of France. It is a perfect alternative to the few recommended industrial seasonings loaded with chemicals and malicious substances for the organism, among which the harmful monosodium glutamate is almost always present. It is composed of a mixture of dried and ground aromatic herbs which brings beneficial substances to the body. They give a delicious touch to the preparations, enhancing their flavor making them more appetizing. The composition of the mixture groups thyme, marjoram, oregano, rosemary, basil, fennel, chervil, tarragon, bay leaf, savory, or lavender, etc.

---

[16] EGW. Counsels on Diet and Foods, 349
[17] Identical.

- **Italian Seasoning or Italian Herbs:** It is another natural seasoning based on a cocktail of dried culinary plants. The preparation consists of marjoram, oregano, thyme, rosemary, savory, basil and sage. The touch of flavor and the contribution of good properties that this seasoning gives to many of my dishes is very convenient and extremely exquisite.

- **Nutritional yeast:** Nutritional yeast flakes are made from inactive yeasts. It's delicious nutty and cheese flavor makes it irresistible to even the most demanding palates. It provides one of the richest sources of vitamin B and trace elements. In addition, it provides proteins of high biological value, key minerals such as zinc, selenium, magnesium, chromium and iron, enzymes and lecithins. It is used as a condiment, as a substitute for traditional cheese, to make vegan butters and mayonnaise, and can be put on pasta, rice, salads, vegetables, meats, or can even be consumed as a nutritional supplement.

- **Vegetable oil:** All the vegetable oils proposed in the different recipes must be in their virgin state, that is, they must be organic. The organic term means two things: first, that the ingredients used to make the oil has not been obtained by genetic manipulation, and, secondly, that it has not been cultivated by traditional methods that use chemical pesticides. On the other hand, these oils are extracted by mechanical and non-chemical processes that usually include petroleum-derived components that are totally toxic and acidifying for the body. Organic means completely natural. Refined oils are not natural, they are not healthy and are a danger to people's health, so it is wise to discard them completely.

- **Carob flour:** Carob is the fruit of the carob tree, which belongs to the legume family. It is a natural substitute for chocolate. From the carob bean a chocolate substitute is prepared, and that, unlike this one, is sweet in nature, since it has fifty percent sucrose, glucose and fructose. The carob tree is typical of the Mediterranean area of Europe. Spain is one of its largest producers. In fact, during the Spanish Civil War, carob became the food par excellence during periods of famine. Although it has traditionally been used to feed cattle, the benefits that this pod has for the human body are indisputable since its intake provides carbohydrates (natural sugars), proteins, fibers, minerals, vitamins and fats of excellent quality. It is magnificent as an astringent, diarrheal and antifungal. It has a sequestering effect that delays the absorption of lipids and carbohydrates. In addition, it has a volumizing effect, which allows to increase stomach repletion and prolongs the feeling of satiety, and a laxative and emollient effect. It is excellent for treating gastritis, gastroduodenal ulcer and childhood vomiting. It is laxative and adjuvant in treatments of overweight, diabetes and hyperlipemia, and is recommended to prevent the onset of arteriosclerosis. The texture of carob flour is very similar to the powdered chocolate, and it has almost identical flavor, therefore, it can be used in the same way in which the popular chocolate is used: in ice cream, milkshakes, milks, custard, cookies, etc.

- Spirulina Seaweed: It is an extremely nutritious and detoxifying seaweed. Due to its outstanding properties, it is consumed as a nutritional supplement even by astronauts. Spirulina is considered a superfood because there is no other food on the face of the Earth that has as much concentration of protein of plant origin as that found in this blessed seaweed. This seaweed, considered by many as miraculous, is a protein concentrate of high biological quality and other components with stimulating, purifying and regenerating properties. Because of its richness in chlorophyll it is a great blood detoxifier, and its high nutritional value has made it a superfood recognized by the United Nations to combat anemia and malnutrition. Spirulina contains chlorophyll, high biological value proteins, vitamins, the main minerals, essential fatty acids, nucleic acids (DNA and RDN), polysaccharides and an endless spectrum of antioxidants. Although it contains vitamin B12, its consumption does not increase the level of this vitamin in the blood since it does not have the bioactive format that the body needs to absorb it.

- Tempeh: Is a soy derivative very rich in vegetable proteins, calcium, heart-healthy fats and isoflavones, which in addition to being an ally of vegetarian and vegan cuisine, is very beneficial for health. It is a product rich in beneficial bacteria to the intestinal microbiota made from fermented soybeans. When talking about fermented foods, the image of rotten foods may come to mind, but the fermentation to which I refer has nothing to do with that concept. There are ferments that enhance health and life. They are healthy ferments, and tempeh is one of them. The intake of properly fermented foods can improve the functioning of the gastrointestinal tract and the quality and quantity of the bacteria that cohabit inside us because they are rich in good or friendly intestinal bacteria. The fermented ones help digest and replenish the bacteria that colonize the intestinal flora. Tempeh is considered a probiotic food. That is a food that contains live bacteria that contribute to the balance of the intestinal flora and that also boost the immune system. You just must consider one detail: make sure they come from organic and non-transgenic soy.

- Soy sauce: "The traditional soy sauce is a common ingredient in vegetarian and vegan cuisine. It is a byproduct of soy that is used as a condiment and that gives a special touch to recipes. A natural soy sauce should have among its ingredients soybeans and purified water, nothing more. However, it is common to find that not a few commercial brands in making the popular sauce have included monosodium glutamate among its components. When buying this sauce, you should read the list of ingredients, and discard those that have not been made with organic soybeans and purified water exclusively."[18] It is recommended to make sure that the soy sauce has organic origin.

- Fruits of the forest (berries in English): The fruits of the forest are small edible fruits of the berry type. In common language, fruits of the forest are called small, sweet or acidic, juicy and intensely colored fruits obtained from wild shrubs. Traditionally, they were not cultivated, but grew in wild shrubs. The story goes that in the medieval world the forests belonged to the feudal lord, and the fruits of the forest or berries that grew there could be collected by the peasants, but, in return, they had to pay to the lord for taking them. Nowadays, for example, blueberries, blackberries, red cranberry, cherry, raspberries, strawberries, red currants, white currants, blackcurrants, and rose hips (not raw, but in jams and infusions), are classified as forest fruits. In addition to being delicious, the fruits of the forest have multiple medicinal properties because they are rich in phytochemicals such as flavonoids, anthocyanins and tannins, located mainly in the skin and seeds of these small fruits. Many fruits of the forest have antioxidant pigments and a high capacity for free radical absorption, which are the number one enemy of the cells. Their color gives them a series of irresistible characteristics and qualities associated with the presence of various substances that promote cardiovascular prevention and anti-aging properties.

- Coconut sugar: It is extracted from the sweet nectar of the flowers of the coconut palm tree. Once collected, the sap is cooked over moderate heat to evaporate moisture and excess of water. The sap is 80% water, 15% sugar and 5% minerals, so heat is used to evaporate water. When heated, the sap changes color and goes from being a translucent liquid to a dense, dark brown substance, until it crystallizes and turns into coconut sugar. Coconut sugar has a low glycemic index. The low glycemic index makes it an ideal natural sweetener for diabetics, people interested in weight loss, or simply for those looking for a healthier alternative to standard sweeteners. Coconut sugar contains essential minerals such as potassium, magnesium, sulfur, zinc and iron, as well as vitamins C, B3, B6, B1 and B2. Coconut sugar has 25% more potassium than bananas. In addition to being low glycemic, it can help reduce blood cholesterol levels. It is rich in macro   micronutrients. Its flavor is like caramel.

- Date sugar: It is a natural and healthy sweetener and a good alternative to white or brown sugar because it is the own fruit dehydrated and grinded. It is produced from dehydrated and crystallized dates. It is the powder of dried dates. This makes it not a sugar that dissolves or melts with heat, but it has many culinary applications

---

[18]Nely Helena Acosta Carrillo. Excerpted from the book BACK TO EDEN: A HEALTHY FOOD GUIDE.

to sweeten healthily. Date sugar contains high doses of calories, but unlike white or brown sugar, it provides minerals, vitamins and fiber that help maintain a good intestinal transit because facilitate the elimination of waste substances from the body. It is very sweet and minimally processed, which makes it more natural than other known alternatives.

- Sea or Himalayan salt: In all recipes that require it, either sea salt or Himalayan salt is used. Never salt refined. Salt is the only rock that is edible for humans and is possibly the oldest and cheapest seasoning. But refined salt is not the same as sea salt. The first only has sodium, the perfect ingredient to damage cardiovascular health. The second has all the minerals that the body needs. Nothing refined is good. Refining means impoverishment of the original material, and nothing impoverished feeds. Refined or degenerated salt, which is the one used by most people, is a poison, because it is practically sodium chloride and does not provide the necessary minerals for blood, and, in addition, it is highly acidifying. In contrast, sea salt not only has all the minerals in the periodic table, but it is also poor in sodium. The same goes for rock salts such as the Himalayan or the Alps salt. Taken to the right quantities these salts are an injection of life for the blood and bring energy and vitality to our body. A person weighing 70 kilograms (154 pounds) should consume about 12-14 grams of salt daily. Quality salt provides alkalinity and the health of the whole body depends on the alkalinity.

And speaking of ingredients, in this book of vegan recipes there are some preparations that include honey. "Regarding honey, it should be noted that some people consider it as a food of animal origin and others do not. However, honey really is not a product of animal origin, although an animal - the bee - intervenes in its elaboration. Honey is made from a vegetable material, flower nectar, and the contact with the insect's saliva transforms the nectar into the final product. The only thing they do is transfer the nectar in their mouth and place it in the hive. It is impossible to consider honey as an animal derived food like milk or eggs that are products generated within the animal, and, consequently, loaded with their toxins."[19] If you are in the group of vegan people who consider honey as a product of animal origin, then you should substitute that ingredient for natural sweeteners that do not pose health risks.

And don't worry, you should know that all the ingredients that are part of the different proposals presented in this book can be purchased in conventional markets or in natural products stores.

---

[19] Nely Helena Acosta Carrillo. Extracted from the book DIET, SPIRITUALITY AND SALVATION.

Unlike traditional cooking, this style of cooking does not depend on exact amounts of ingredients to make a recipe look good. Being all-natural products, there is a margin of play that does not exist in the other type of cuisine. For example, if you are going to make almond and prunes butter, you can put more or a smaller number of prunes, depending on the degree of sweetness and the texture you want to achieve. It is always good, even if you put more or put less. That means that the amounts of ingredients proposed in each of the recipes in this book do not have to be exact. You can move from more to less, depending on your personal taste.

To prepare the recipes, and since they were based on mixtures of different products with more or less hardness level, a powerful food processor, a Nutribullet, a Ninja equipment or any other that are appropriate for these requirements are needed.

Finally, it should be clarified that both, butters and mayonnaises, if not consumed at the moment, should be kept in the refrigerator and in glass jars conveniently clean and with a lid. Keeping in mind that we are talking about natural products, without chemical preservatives of any kind, the storage time should not exceed seven days, that is, one week. Besides, it should be noted that all recipes can be used in the same way that traditional recipes of mayonnaise, butters and margarines are usually used: with whole wheat bread or biscuits, to accompany rice, pasta, or boiled or griddle vegetables, etc.

With the help of God, you and your family can enjoy these delicacies that are not only nutritious, healthy and very easy to prepare, but also, in most cases, extremely economical.

And as the French say, it only remains to wish you

Coconut oil and olive oil butter

Ingredients
(1 medium cup)

½ medium cup of coconut oil

½ medium cup of extra virgin olive oil

1 tablespoon of nutritional yeast

A pinch of sea salt

Directions

Put both oils in an appropriate pot and heat them over low heat until they mixed. Add salt and stir. Put the mixture in the small Nutribullet cup, or failing that, in a glass container, and refrigerate until it acquires a solid appearance, like a thick cream. Remove from the refrigerator, add the nutritional yeast and beat the mixture, either in the Nutribullet, in a blender or in a food processor. Beat until the mixture reaches twice its initial size. Empty the contents into the molds chosen and refrigerate to solidify them, as shown in the photo. Remove from the molds and store in the refrigerator in a glass container. This basic recipe can be enriched by adding garlic, onion, chives, coriander or parsley, seaweed, etc.

Cashew and spinach butter

INGREDIENTS (1 MEDIUM CUP)

1 medium cup of raw cashews soaked in pure water for at least 4 hours. Cashews are also known as caju, merey, caguil, pepa or merey.

1 large handful of fresh and washed spinach

1 pinch of sea or Himalayan salt

1 medium lemon juice

Soak water to facilitate the emulsion of the mixture. The amount depends on the texture you want.

DIRECTIONS

Put all the ingredients in the Nutribullet or food processor and mix until a fine and homogeneous texture is achieved, as shown in the photo. Keep or serve.

Sunflower seed butter

Ingredients
(1 medium cup)

1 medium cup of sunflower seeds soaked in pure water for at least 4 hours

1 clove of garlic peeled and crushed

1½-1 medium lemon juice

A pinch of Himalayan salt

3 sprigs of fresh cut coriander

Soak water to facilitate the emulsion of the mixture. The amount depends on the texture you want.

Directions

Put all the ingredients in the Nutribullet or food processor and mix until a fine and homogeneous texture is achieved, as shown in the photo. Keep or serve.

Pumpkin seed butter

Ingredients (1 medium cup)

1 medium cup of pumpkin seeds soaked in pure water for at least 4 hours

½ fresh cut medium tomato

1 clove of garlic peeled and crushed

1 tablespoon of extra-virgin olive oil

1 teaspoon of dried oregano

A pinch of sea salt

Soak water to facilitate the emulsion of the mixture. The amount depends on the texture you want.

Directions

Put all the ingredients in the Nutribullet or food processor and mix until a fine and homogeneous texture is achieved, as shown in the photo. Keep or serve.

Pistachio butter

Ingredients (1 medium cup)

1 medium cup of pistachios soaked in pure water for at least 4 hours

A pinch of sea or Himalayan salt

Soak water to facilitate the emulsion of the mixture. The amount depends on the texture you want.

Directions

Put all the ingredients in the Nutribullet or food processor and mix until a fine and homogeneous texture is achieved, as shown in the photo. Keep or serve.

Chickpea butter

INGREDIENTS (1 MEDIUM CUP)

1 medium cup of cooked and drained chickpeas

1-2 peeled and crushed garlic cloves

1 tablespoon of walnut or extra virgin olive oil

A pinch of Himalayan salt

A pinch of Italian Seasoning or Italian Herbs

1 medium lemon juice

DIRECTIONS

This recipe allows to take advantage of leftover chickpeas from a meal. Only the grains are used, but a small amount of the cooking broth should be reserved in case it is necessary to add it to the mixture and be able to process them without excessive drying. Put all the ingredients in the Nutribullet or food processor and mix until a fine and homogeneous texture is achieved, as shown in the photo. Keep or serve.

Tofu and tempeh butter

Ingredients
(1 medium cup)

½ box of extra firm organic tofu standard size diced

1 package of tempeh standard size

4 tablespoons of soy sauce

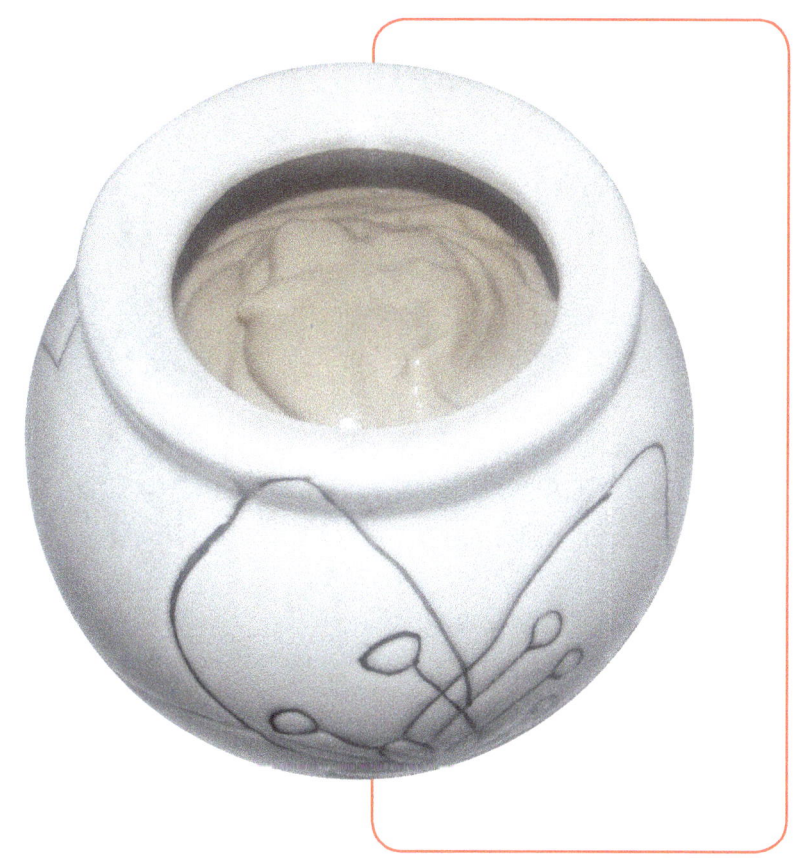

Directions

Put all the ingredients in the Nutribullet or food processor and mix until a fine and homogeneous texture is achieved, as shown in the photo. If necessary, in order to facilitate mixing, add 2-3 tablespoons of the water in which the tofu comes. Keep or serve.

Dried tomato butter

Ingredients (1 medium cup)

1 cup of dried tomatoes soaked in pure water for at least 4 hours. With soaking they double their size and the meat becomes noticeably soft.

½ medium cup of almonds soaked in pure water for at least 4 hours

1-2 garlic cloves peeled and crushed

1 tablespoon of extra-virgin olive oil

A pinch of dried oregano

A pinch of sea or Himalayan salt

Soak water to facilitate the emulsion of the mixture. The amount depends on the texture you want.

Directions

Put all the ingredients in the Nutribullet or food processor and mix until a fine and homogeneous texture is achieved, as shown in the photo. Keep or serve.

Eggplant butter

Ingredients
(1 medium cup)

1 small eggplant

1 clove of garlic, peeled and crushed

2 tablespoons of tomato sauce, preferably homemade

A pinch of Provence herbs

1 tablespoon of extra-virgin olive oil

A pinch of sea salt

Directions

Wash, slice and grill the eggplant on the grill or in the oven. Let cool and remove the skin. Put all the ingredients in the Nutribullet or food processor and mix until a fine and homogeneous texture is achieved, as shown in the photo. Keep or serve.

Zucchini and onions butter

Ingredients
(1 medium cup)

1 large zucchini

1 medium onion

3 tablespoons of vegan natural yogurt

A few sprigs of fresh mint

A pinch of Himalayan salt

1 tablespoon of extra-virgin olive oil

Directions

Wash, peel and steam the zucchini and the onion, until they are soft, but with the firm dough. Let cool. Put all the ingredients in the Nutribullet or food processor and mix until a fine and homogeneous texture is achieved, as shown in the photo. Keep or serve.

Green olives butter

Ingredients
(1 medium cup)

1 medium can of green boneless olives preserved in water and salt (not in vinegar)

1 clove of garlic peeled and crushed

A pinch of sea salt

A pinch of Provence herbs

Directions

Drain the olives, put them in a strainer under the tap and wash them thoroughly with pure water in order to remove as many preservatives as possible. Put all the ingredients in the Nutribullet or food processor and mix. If you want to get a fine texture you should mix for a longer time. If a thicker texture is desired, as is the case with this recipe, the processing time should be minimal. Keep or serve.

Avocado and dried tomato butter

Ingredients
(1 medium cup)

½ medium ripe avocado
¼ cut small purple onion
½ cut medium red pepper
A cut sprig of coriander and parsley
½ cut medium ripe tomato
1 small cup of dried tomatoes soaked in pure water for at least 4 hours
½ medium lemon juice
A pinch of sea or Himalayan salt
To decorate 3 black olives preserved in salted water, and not in vinegar

Directions

In an appropriate container, crush the avocado pulp with a fork. Add the rest of the ingredients and mix until achieving a texture like the one in the photo. Decorate with the black olives. Keep or serve.

Brazil nut and apricots butter

Ingredients
(1 medium cup)

½ medium cup of raw Brazil nuts soaked in pure water for at least 4 hours

1 medium cup of dried apricots soaked in pure water for at least 4 hours

Soak water to facilitate the emulsion of the mixture. The amount depends on the texture you want.

Directions

Put all the ingredients in the Nutribullet or food processor and mix until a fine and homogeneous texture is achieved, as shown in the photo. Keep or serve.

Almond and prunes butter

Ingredients (1 medium cup)

½ medium cup of raw almonds soaked in pure water for at least 4 hours

1 medium cup of prunes soaked in pure water for at least 4 hours

Soak water to facilitate the emulsion of the mixture. The amount depends on the texture you want.

Directions

Put all the ingredients in the Nutribullet or food processor and mix until a fine and homogeneous texture is achieved, as shown in the photo. Keep or serve.

Peanut and honey butter

Ingredients
(1 medium cup)

1 medium cup of raw peanuts soaked in pure water for at least 4 hours

Organic honey to your taste

Soak water to facilitate the emulsion of the mixture. The amount depends on the texture you want.

Directions

Put all the ingredients in the Nutribullet or food processor and mix until a fine and homogeneous texture is achieved, as shown in the photo. Keep or serve.

Peanut and raisins butter

INGREDIENTS
(1 MEDIUM CUP)

½ medium cup of raw peanuts soaked in pure water for at least 4 hours

1 medium cup of raisins soaked in pure water for at least 4 hours

Soak water to facilitate the emulsion of the mixture. The amount depends on the texture you want.

DIRECTIONS

Put all the ingredients in the Nutribullet or food processor and mix until a fine and homogeneous texture is achieved, as shown in the photo.
Keep or serve.

Peanut and dates butter

Ingredients
(1 medium cup)

½ medium cup of raw peanuts soaked in pure water for at least 4 hours

1 medium cup of dried dates soaked in pure water for at least 4 hours

Soak water to facilitate the emulsion of the mixture. The amount depends on the texture you want.

Directions

Put all the ingredients in the Nutribullet or food processor and mix until a fine and homogeneous texture is achieved, as shown in the photo.
Keep or serve.

Fig and nut butter

Ingredients
(1 medium cup)

½ medium cup of raw nuts soaked in pure water for at least 4 hours

1 medium cup of dried figs soaked in pure water for at least 4 hours

Soak water to facilitate the emulsion of the mixture. The amount depends on the texture you want.

Directions

Put all the ingredients in the Nutribullet or food processor and mix until a fine and homogeneous texture is achieved, as shown in the photo. Keep or serve.

Hazelnut and pineapple butter

Ingredients
(1 medium cup)

½ medium cup of raw hazelnuts soaked in pure water for at least 4 hours

1 medium cup of dried pineapple soaked in pure water for at least 4 hours

Soak water to facilitate the emulsion of the mixture. The amount depends on the texture you want.

Directions

Put all the ingredients in the Nutribullet or food processor and mix until a fine and homogeneous texture is achieved, as shown in the photo. Keep or serve.

Berries and cashews butter

INGREDIENTS
(1 MEDIUM CUP)

½ medium cup of raw cashews soaked in pure water for at least 4 hours. Cashews are also known as caju, merey, caguil, pepa or merey.

1 cup of dried berries soaked in pure water for at least 4 hours

Soak water to facilitate the emulsion of the mixture. The amount depends on the texture you want.

DIRECTIONS

Put all the ingredients in the Nutribullet or food processor and mix until a fine and homogeneous texture is achieved, as shown in the photo. Keep or serve.

Macadamia nut and dates butter

Ingredients
(1 medium cup)

½ medium cup of raw Macadamia nuts soaked in pure water for at least 4 hours

1 medium cup of dried dates soaked in pure water for at least 4 hours

Soak water to facilitate the emulsion of the mixture. The amount depends on the texture you want.

Directions

Put all the ingredients in the Nutribullet or food processor and mix until a fine and homogeneous texture is achieved, as shown in the photo. Keep or serve.

Chia seed, berries and prunes butter

INGREDIENTS
(1 MEDIUM CUP)

½ medium cup of chia seeds soaked in pure water for at least 4 hours

½ medium cup of dried berries soaked in pure water for at least 4 hours

½ medium cup of dried prunes soaked in pure water for at least 4 hours

Soak water to facilitate the emulsion of the mixture. The amount depends on the texture you want.

DIRECTIONS

Put all the ingredients in the Nutribullet or food processor and mix until a fine and homogeneous texture is achieved, as shown in the photo. Keep or serve.

Dry coconut and sesame butter

Ingredients
(1 medium cup)

½ cup of dried coconut in slices or powder, soaked in pure water for at least 4 hours

1 tablespoon of lightly toasted sesame seeds

1 cup of dried berries soaked in pure water for at least 4 hours
Organic honey to your taste

Soak water to facilitate the emulsion of the mixture. The amount depends on the texture you want.

Directions

Put all the ingredients in the Nutribullet or food processor and mix until a fine and homogeneous texture is achieved, as shown in the photo.
Keep or serve.

Tender coconut meat and carob flour butter

Ingredients
(1 medium cup)

1 medium cup of tender coconut dough

2 tablespoons of carob flour

5-6 tablespoons date sugar

Soak water to facilitate the emulsion of the mixture. The amount depends on the texture you want.

Directions

Put all the ingredients in the Nutribullet or food processor and mix until a fine and homogeneous texture is achieved, as shown in the photo. Keep or serve.

Pumpkin and carob flour butter

Ingredients
(1 medium cup)

¼ medium pumpkin

A small cup of raw peanut soaked in pure water for at least 4 hours

4 tablespoons of coconut sugar

1 pinch of carob flour to decorate

5 carob chips (carob) to decorate

Soak water to facilitate the emulsion of the mixture. The amount depends on the texture you want.

Directions

Wash, cut and steam the pumpkin until it is tender, but with the firm dough. Let cool. Put all the ingredients in the Nutribullet or food processor and mix until a fine and homogeneous texture is achieved, as shown in the photo. Decorate sprinkling the carob flour and placing the chips on the butter. Keep or serve.

Tofu mayonnaise

Ingredients (1 medium cup)

1 box of extra firm organic tofu standard size diced

1 tablespoon of nutritional yeast

2 cloves of garlic peeled and crushed

1 tablespoon of extra-virgin olive oil

1-1½ medium lemon juice

A pinch of sea salt

Directions

Put all the ingredients in the Nutribullet or food processor and mix until a fine and homogeneous texture is achieved, as shown in the photo. If necessary, in order to facilitate mixing, add 2-3 tablespoons of the water in which the tofu comes. Keep or serve.

Tofu and coriander mayonnaise

Ingredients
(1 medium cup)

1 box of extra firm organic tofu standard size diced

2 cloves of garlic peeled and crushed

1 tablespoon of extra-virgin olive oil

1 medium lemon juice

1 cut and washed coriander branch

A pinch of Himalayan salt

Directions

Put all the ingredients in the Nutribullet or food processor and mix until a fine and homogeneous texture is achieved, as shown in the photo. If necessary, in order to facilitate mixing, add 2-3 tablespoons of the water in which the tofu comes. Keep or serve.

Asparagus mayonnaise

Ingredients
(1 medium cup)

12 spears of green Asparagus

½ extra virgin organic tofu box of standard size diced

½ medium lemon juice

A pinch of Himalayan salt

A pinch of Provence herbs

1 tablespoon of extra-virgin olive oil

Directions

Wash and cut the asparagus into medium pieces. Grill or bake in the oven. Let cool. Put all the ingredients in the Nutribullet or food processor and mix until a fine and homogeneous texture is achieved, as shown in the photo. If necessary, in order to facilitate mixing, add 2-3 tablespoons of the water in which the tofu comes. Keep or serve.

Black olives mayonnaise

Ingredients
(1 medium cup)

1 medium can of black boneless olives preserved in water and salt (not in vinegar)

¼ extra virgin organic tofu box of standard size diced

¼ medium raw onion

A pinch of sea salt

A pinch of Italian herbs

Directions

Drain the olives, put them in a strainer under the tap and wash them thoroughly with pure water in order to remove as many preservatives as possible.

Put all the ingredients in the Nutribullet or food processor and mix until a fine and homogeneous texture is achieved, as shown in the photo. Keep or serve.

Fine herbs mayonnaise

INGREDIENTS
(1 MEDIUM CUP)

½ medium cup of raw hazelnuts soaked in pure water for at least 4 hours

4 tablespoons of vegan sour cream

3 cut and washed parsley branches

3 sprigs of cut coriander

6-8 fresh mint leaves

A handful of fresh spinach

1-2 garlic cloves peeled and crushed

Juice of ½-1 medium lemon

A pinch of sea or Himalayan salt

A tablespoon of extra-virgin olive oil

DIRECTIONS

Put all the ingredients in the Nutribullet or food processor and mix until a fine and homogeneous texture is achieved, as shown in the photo. Keep or serve.

Lentil mayonnaise

Ingredients
(1 medium cup)

1 medium cup of cooked and drained lentils

2 tablespoons of almond milk

½ medium raw onion

1 tablespoon of extra-virgin olive oil

1 medium lemon juice

A pinch of Himalayan salt

A pinch of cumin powder

Directions

This recipe allows to take advantage of lentils left over from a meal. Only the grains are used, but a small amount of the cooking broth should be reserved in case it is necessary to add it to the mixture and be able to process them without excessive drying. Put all the ingredients in the Nutribullet or food processor and mix until a fine and homogeneous texture is achieved, as shown in the photo. Keep or serve.

Basil mayonnaise

Ingredients
(1 medium cup)

1 medium cup of raw cashews soaked in pure water for at least 4 hours. Cashews are also known as caju, merey, caguil, pepa or merey.

1 tablespoon of nutritional yeast

A pinch of sea or Himalayan salt

½ clove of garlic peeled and crushed

½ medium lemon juice

8 fresh basil leaves

Soak water to facilitate the emulsion of the of mayonnaise. The amount depends on the texture you want.

Directions

Put all the ingredients in the Nutribullet or food processor and mix until a fine and homogeneous texture is achieved, as shown in the photo. Keep or serve.

Avocado and peppermint mayonnaise

Ingredients (1 medium cup)

1 medium avocado with firm dough

1 tablespoon of nutritional yeast

10 washed and cut leaves of peppermint

1 clove of garlic peeled and crushed

1 medium lemon juice

A pinch of Himalayan salt

Directions

Cut the avocado and extract the dough. Put it in the Nutribullet or food processor together with the rest of the ingredients and mix until a fine and homogeneous texture is achieved, as shown in the photo. Keep or serve.

Avocado and mint mayonnaise

Ingredients
(1 medium cup)

1 medium avocado with firm dough

10 washed and cut mint leaves

¼ medium purple onion

1 medium lemon juice

A pinch of sea salt

Directions

Cut the avocado and extract the dough. Put it in the Nutribullet or food processor together with the rest of the ingredients and mix until a fine and homogeneous texture is achieved, as shown in the photo. Keep or serve.

Avocado and coriander mayonnaise

INGREDIENTS
(1 MEDIUM CUP)

1 medium avocado with firm dough

6-7 washed and cut sprigs coriander

¼ medium white onion

1 medium lemon juice

A pinch of sea salt

DIRECTIONS

Cut the avocado and extract the dough. Put it in the Nutribullet or food processor together with the rest of the ingredients and mix until a fine and homogeneous texture is achieved, as shown in the photo. Keep or serve.

Almond mayonnaise

Ingredients
(1 medium cup)

1 medium cup of raw almonds soaked in pure water for at least 4 hours

1 tablespoon of nutritional yeast

1 clove of garlic peeled and crushed

A pinch of sea salt

Soak water to facilitate the emulsion of mayonnaise. The amount depends on the texture you want.

Directions

Put all the ingredients in the Nutribullet or food processor and mix until a fine and homogeneous texture is achieved, as shown in the photo. Keep or serve.

Cashew mayonnaise

Ingredients
(1 medium cup)

1 medium cup of raw cashews soaked in pure water for at least 4 hours. Cashews are also known as caju, merey, caguil, pepa or merey.

1 medium lemon juice

A pinch of Himalayan salt

Soak water to facilitate the emulsion of mayonnaise. The amount depends on the texture you want.

Directions

Put all the ingredients in the Nutribullet or food processor and mix until a fine and homogeneous texture is achieved, as shown in the photo. Keep or serve.

Cashew and spirulina mayonnaise

Ingredients (1 medium cup)

1 medium cup of raw cashews soaked in pure water for at least 4 hours. Cashews are also known as caju, merey, caguil, pepa or merey.

1 medium lemon juice

1 tablespoon of spirulina seaweed powder

1 clove of garlic peeled and crushed

A pinch of Himalayan salt

1 pinch of thyme powder

Soak water to facilitate the emulsion of mayonnaise. The amount depends on the texture you want.

Directions

Put all the ingredients in the Nutribullet or food processor and mix until a fine and homogeneous texture is achieved, as shown in the photo. Keep or serve.

Spinach and Brazil nut mayonnaise

Ingredients
(1 medium cup)

1 medium cup of raw Brazil nuts soaked in pure water for at least 4 hours

1 medium cup of fresh spinach

1 tablespoon of avocado oil

1 clove of garlic peeled and crushed
1 medium lemon juice

A pinch of sea or Himalayan salt

Soak water to facilitate the emulsion of mayonnaise. The amount depends on the texture you want.

Directions

Put all the ingredients in the Nutribullet or food processor and mix until a fine and homogeneous texture is achieved, as shown in the photo.
Keep or serve.

Red peppers and almonds mayonnaise

Ingredients
(1 medium cup)

3 raw red peppers

½ medium cup of raw almonds soaked in water for at least 4 hours

1 clove of garlic peeled and crushed

2 tablespoons of nutritional yeast

Juice of 1 small lemon

A pinch of sea or Himalayan salt

Soak water to facilitate the emulsion of mayonnaise. The amount depends on the texture you want.

Directions

Put all the ingredients in the Nutribullet or food processor and mix until a fine and homogeneous texture is achieved, as shown in the photo.
Keep or serve.

Zucchini and pumpkin seeds mayonnaise

Ingredients
(1 medium cup)

1 medium zucchini

2 tablespoons of pumpkin seeds soaked in pure water for at least 4 hours

1-2 garlic cloves peeled and crushed

A few sprigs of fresh parsley

A few sprigs of fresh basil

A pinch of sea or Himalayan salt

1 tablespoon of extra-virgin olive oil

Directions

Wash and steam the zucchini until it is soft, but with the firm dough. Let cool. Put all the ingredients in the Nutribullet or food processor and mix until a fine and homogeneous texture is achieved, as shown in the photo. Keep or serve.

Zucchini and oregano mayonnaise

Ingredients
(1 medium cup)

1 medium zucchini

1 tablespoon of nutritional yeast

1 teaspoon of dried oregano powder

A pinch of sea or Himalayan salt

1 tablespoon of extra-virgin olive oil

Directions

Wash and steam the zucchini until it is soft, but with the firm dough. Let cool. Put all the ingredients in the Nutribullet or food processor and mix until a fine and homogeneous texture is achieved, as shown in the photo. Keep or serve.

Soft yogurt mayonnaise

**INGREDIENTS
(1 MEDIUM CUP)**

1 cup of unsweetened natural vegan yogurt

½ medium cup of raw walnuts soaked in water for at least 4 hours

Juice of ½-1 medium lemon

5 coriander sprigs

1-2 garlic cloves peeled and crushed

A pinch of sea or Himalayan salt

DIRECTIONS

Put all the ingredients in the Nutribullet or food processor and mix until a fine and homogeneous texture is achieved, as shown in the photo. Keep or serve.

Garlic mayonnaise

Ingredients
(1 medium cup)

1 cup of raw Macadamia nuts soaked in water for at least 4 hours

3-4 crushed garlic cloves

1 lemon juice

A pinch of sea or Himalayan salt

Soak water to facilitate the emulsion of mayonnaise. The amount depends on the texture you want.

Directions

Put all the ingredients in the Nutribullet or food processor and mix until a fine and homogeneous texture is achieved, as shown in the photo.
Keep or serve.

Beet mayonnaise

Ingredients (1 medium cup)

1 large beet

1-2 garlic cloves peeled and crushed

1 medium lemon juice

A pinch of sea or Himalayan salt

A pinch of Provence herbs

1 teaspoon of organic coconut oil

1 teaspoon of raw sesame to decorate

Directions

Wash and steam the beet. Let cool. Remove the skin and cut into small pieces. Put all the ingredients in the Nutribullet or food processor and mix until a fine and homogeneous texture is achieved, as shown in the photo. Decorate with sesame seeds. Keep or serve.

Tomato mayonnaise

Ingredients
(1 medium cup)

2 medium ripe tomatoes
with a firm dough

½ medium cup of raw almonds soaked in water for at least 4 hours

A handful of raw celery leaves

3 cut sprigs of parsley

1 clove of garlic peeled and crushed

A pinch of sea or Himalayan salt

Directions

Put all the ingredients in the Nutribullet or food processor and mix until a fine and homogeneous texture is achieved, as shown in the photo.
Keep or serve.

Carrot mayonnaise

Ingredients (1 medium cup)

2 large carrots

1 medium potato

A pinch of sea or Himalayan salt

A pinch of Provence herbs

1 tablespoon of extra-virgin olive oil

½ medium raw onion

1 medium lemon juice

Directions

Wash, peel, cut and boil the potato and carrot until tender. Let cool. Place them in the Nutribullet or in a powerful mixer with the rest of the ingredients. Mix. If the mixture is very thick, add some cooking water and blend until it forms a cream with a texture like mayonnaise, as shown in the photo. Keep or serve.

Potato and radish mayonnaise

Ingredients
(1 medium cup)

1 medium cooked potato

1 clove of garlic peeled and crushed

4 raw radishes in slices

1 tablespoon of nutritional yeast

1 tablespoon of extra-virgin olive oil

A pinch of sea or Himalayan salt

A pinch of fresh or dried oregano

1 medium lemon juice

2-3 tablespoons of cooking water to facilitate mayonnaise emulsion

Directions

Wash, peel and cook the potato in water until it softens. Let it cool. Put all the ingredients in the Nutribullet or in a powerful mixer and process. If the preparation is very compact, it can be softened by adding more cooking water to achieve a good consistency and a fine and homogeneous texture, as shown in the photo. Keep or serve.

Celery and walnut mayonnaise

Ingredients
(1 medium cup)

2-3 large branches of celery with it leaf

1 medium cup of raw nuts soaked in pure water for at least 4 hours

2 coriander sprigs

1 clove of garlic peeled and crushed

Juice of ½-1 medium lemon

A pinch of Himalayan salt

A tablespoon of unrefined sunflower oil

Directions

Wash and cut the celery into small pieces. Put it in the Nutribullet or food processor together with the rest of the ingredients and mix until a fine and homogeneous texture is achieved, as shown in the photo. Keep or serve.

Cauliflower mayonnaise

**INGREDIENTS
(1 MEDIUM CUP)**

1 small cauliflower

½ small cup of almond milk

1-2 clove of garlic peeled and crushed

1 medium lemon juice

4-5 tablespoons of nutritional yeast

A pinch of sea salt

A pinch of Provence herbs

1 tablespoon of extra-virgin olive oil

DIRECTIONS

Wash, cut and steam the cauliflower until smooth, but with firm dough. Let cool. Put all the ingredients in the Nutribullet or in a food processor and mix until a fine and homogeneous texture is achieved, as shown in the photo. Keep or serve.

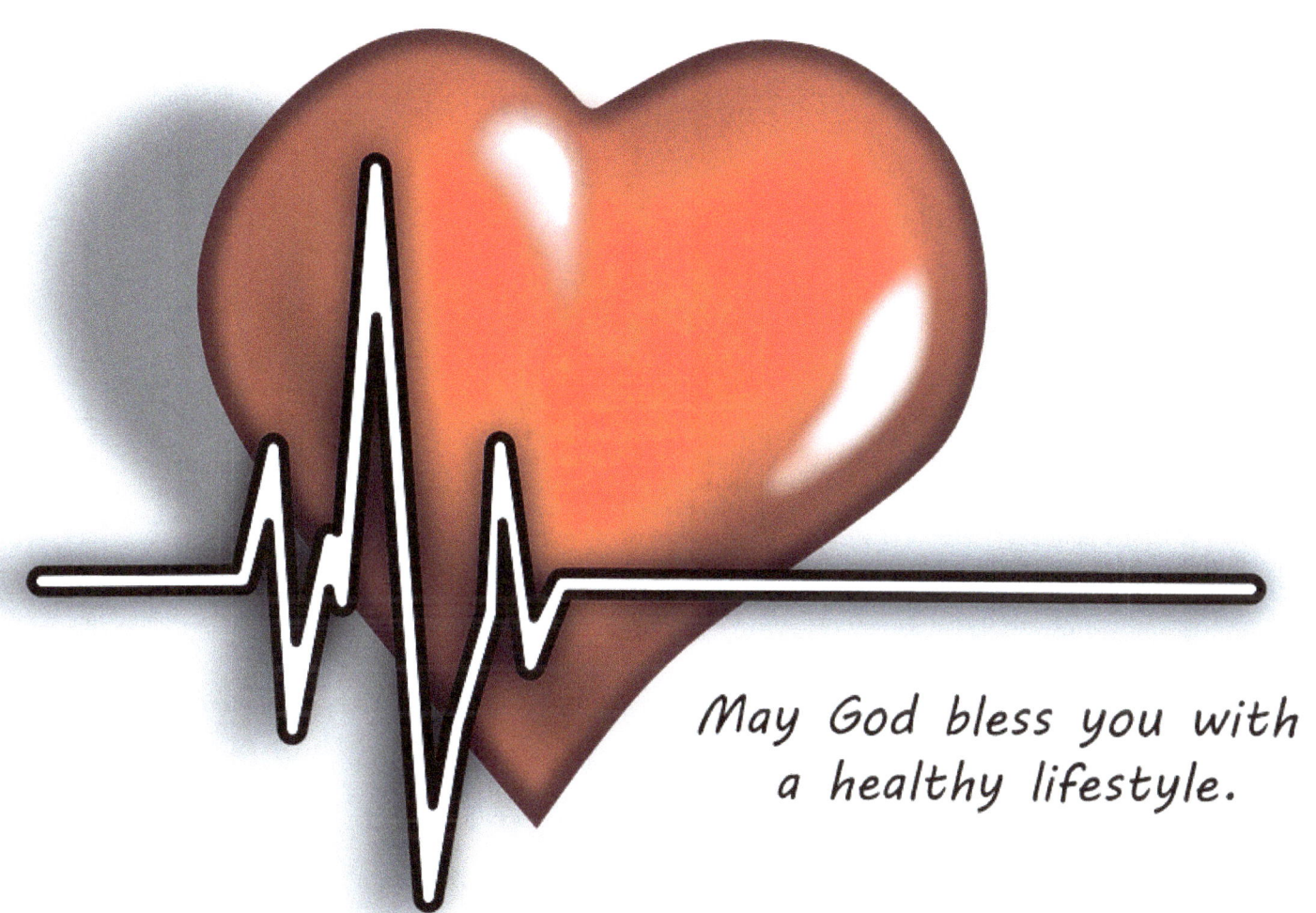

May God bless you with a healthy lifestyle.

Books available from the writer, speaker, and YouTuber Nely Helena Acosta Carrillo

In Spanish

A book that highlights the close relationship between physical habits, including food, correct spiritual perception and the promise of salvation given by Jesus Christ, our Savior.

It is not a simple healthy food recipe book. It is much more than that: a guide that takes you by the hand and makes the path of transition to a proper lifestyle lighter.

This book is an excerpt from the full version of BACK TO EDEN: A HEALTHY FOOD GUIDE, with 100 healthy, economical, exquisite and easy-to-make recipes. All preparations have been thought to free you from a enslaving culinary lifestyle, to delight you and to feed you properly.

A book full of healthy, delicious and nutritious options of butters and mayonnaises that translate into an excellent substitute for traditional recipes whose ingredients are an attack on human health. Do not stop eating mayonnaise and butters. Just look for smarter options. This book offers a wide range of different alternatives.

DVD's available from the writer, speaker, and YouTuber Nely Helena Acosta Carrillo

A three-hour Vegan Cooking Course that was recorded live in Laguna Niguel, California and that not only shares healthy food recipes, but also provides tons of essential information to enjoy a healthy life.

Ways of contact to purchase books and DVD's
(Forma de contacto para adquirir libros y DVD's)

Phone number (número de teléfono): 786.356.6779
E-mail: nelyacostaquinonespublications@gmail.com

Butters, margarines and traditional mayonnaises, whether homemade or industrial, have among their ingredients elements that, now a days, medical science has shown to be an attack against people's health. Concerning this there are bad news and also good news. The bad news is that, although millions of people around the world consume them regularly, the wisest decision is to abandon their consumption if you want to avoid diseases. The good news is that there are healthy, economical, easy to prepare and nutritionally excellent alternatives that can be used to satisfy the desire to eat these types of preparations. The book you have in your hands, in the first place, explains both the inconveniences of the ingredients of these recipes in their traditional version, as well as their elaboration process, and, secondly, it offers you 50 alternative suggestions of vegan butters and mayonnaises as ideal substitutes free of animal proteins or fats, of refined and industrialized "foods" or of any other type of "food" harmful to people's health. Without a doubt your senses will be stunned by so much nutrition and deliciousness.

BON APPETIT

www.ingramcontent.com/pod-product-compliance
Lightning Source LLC
Chambersburg PA
CBHW060426010526
44118CB00017B/2373